Bipolar 2 Workbook

A PRACTICAL WORKSHEETS TO HELP MANAGE MOODS IN PEOPLE WITH BIPOLAR DISORDER TYPE 2

Copyright 2021 © MESLOUB IHEB

ISBN: 9798483159766

Delusions and Hallucinations, Paranoia Reflexions Tracker

Take care of your mental health. Know when to seek help.

(Symptom) or (Behavior)	Psychological and Physiological Reflexes
1	2
3	4
5	6
6	6
6	6
6	6

OVERCOMING BIPOLAR SYMPTOMS

IN THIS TABLE, TRY TO UNDERSTAND AND EXPLAIN THE EPISODES OF MANIA, DELUSIONS AND HALLUCINATIONS THAT OCCUR TO YOU FROM TIME TO TIME.
STATE THE EFFECT THEY HAVE ON YOUR FEELINGS AND ACTIONS, WHAT COPING SKILLS DO YOU THINK WORK WHEN YOU USE THEM, AND HOW SUCCESSFUL ARE YOU IN APPLYING THOSE SKILLS?

MANIC - DELUSIONS- HALLUCINATIONS EPISODES	COPING SKILLS USED OR PREVENTION METHODS
	👍
	✋

DAILY BIPOLAR MOOD CYCLE

Instructions: Think about your day from start to finish. Color the first square to express your feelings each time of the day. Next, write a word that reflects your feelings, and draw in the circle a picture of your face that reflects your feelings at that moment.

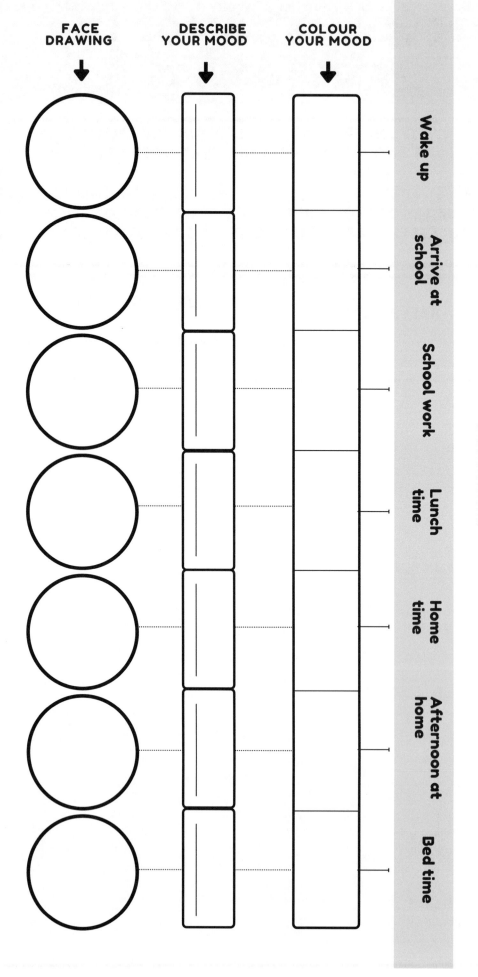

FACE DRAWING

DESCRIBE YOUR MOOD

COLOUR YOUR MOOD

Wake up

Arrive at school

School work

Lunch time

Home time

Afternoon at home

Bed time

BIPOLAR DISORDER
DBT WORKSHEET

MARK FEELINGS AND EPISODES OF JOY, EXCITEMENT, STRENGTH, OR ANY UNUSUAL TALENT THAT WERE PART OF YOUR DAY.

⊘ —— : ——

⊘ —— : ——

⊘ —— : ——

ONE WAY TO MAKE TOMORROW BETTER

Daily Mood Checker ✓

ANGRY	☐
ANNOYED	☐
ANXIOUS	☐
ASHAMED	☐
AWKWARD	☐
BRAVE	☐
CALM	☐
CHEERFUL	☐
CHILL	☐
CONFUSED	☐
DISCOURAGED	☐
DISTRACTED	☐
EMBARRASSED	☐
EXCITED	☐
FRIENDLY	☐
GUILTY	☐
HAPPY	☐
HOPEFUL	☐
LONELY	☐
LOVED	☐
NERVOUS	☐
OFFENDED	☐
SCARED	☐
THOUGHTFUL	☐
TIRED	☐
UNCOMFORTABLE	☐
UNSURE	☐

CHALLENGING BIPOLAR WORKSHEEYT

Date :

Identify feelings, episodes of joy, excitement, strength or any unusual talent that was part of your day , also things can you do to prevent a full-blown (manic - depressive) episode

_____

_____

_____

_____

_____

_____

_____

_____

_____

_____

_____

_____

_____

Delusions and Hallucinations, Paranoia Reflexions Tracker

Take care of your mental health. Know when to seek help.

(Symptom) or (Behavior)	Psychological and Physiological Reflexes
1	2
3	4
5	6
6	6
6	6
6	6

OVERCOMING BIPOLAR SYMPTOMS

IN THIS TABLE, TRY TO UNDERSTAND AND EXPLAIN THE EPISODES OF MANIA, DELUSIONS AND HALLUCINATIONS THAT OCCUR TO YOU FROM TIME TO TIME.
STATE THE EFFECT THEY HAVE ON YOUR FEELINGS AND ACTIONS, WHAT COPING SKILLS DO YOU THINK WORK WHEN YOU USE THEM, AND HOW SUCCESSFUL ARE YOU IN APPLYING THOSE SKILLS?

MANIC - DELUSIONS- HALLUCINATIONS EPISODES	COPING SKILLS USED OR PREVENTION METHODS
	👍
	✋

DAILY BIPOLAR MOOD CYCLE

Instructions: Think about your day from start to finish. Color the first square to express your feelings each time of the day. Next, write a word that reflects your feelings, and draw in the circle a picture of your face that reflects your feelings at that moment.

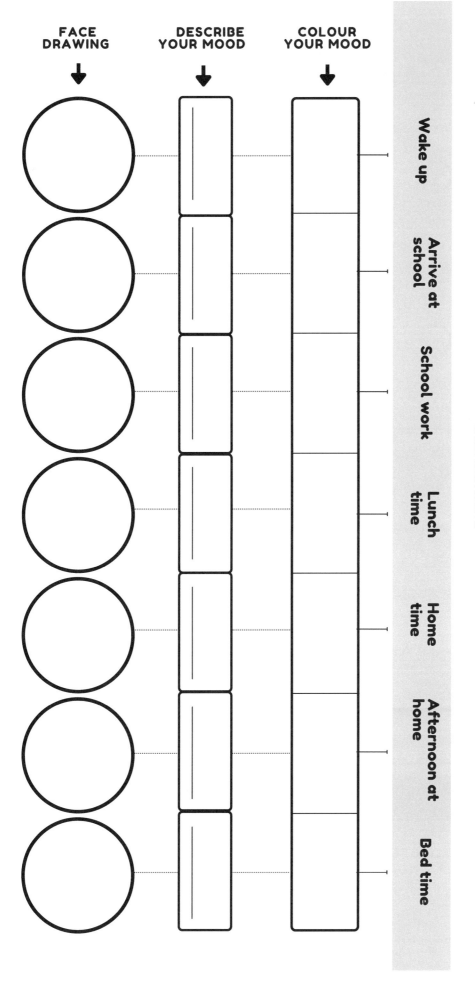

FACE DRAWING

DESCRIBE YOUR MOOD

COLOUR YOUR MOOD

Wake up

Arrive at school

School work

Lunch time

Home time

Afternoon at home

Bed time

BIPOLAR DISORDER
DBT WORKSHEET

MARK FEELINGS AND EPISODES OF JOY, EXCITEMENT, STRENGTH, OR ANY UNUSUAL TALENT THAT WERE PART OF YOUR DAY.

✓ ___ : ___

✓ ___ : ___

✓ ___ : ___

ONE WAY TO MAKE TOMORROW BETTER

Daily Mood Checker ✔

ANGRY	☐
ANNOYED	☐
ANXIOUS	☐
ASHAMED	☐
AWKWARD	☐
BRAVE	☐
CALM	☐
CHEERFUL	☐
CHILL	☐
CONFUSED	☐
DISCOURAGED	☐
DISTRACTED	☐
EMBARRASSED	☐
EXCITED	☐
FRIENDLY	☐
GUILTY	☐
HAPPY	☐
HOPEFUL	☐
LONELY	☐
LOVED	☐
NERVOUS	☐
OFFENDED	☐
SCARED	☐
THOUGHTFUL	☐
TIRED	☐
UNCOMFORTABLE	☐
UNSURE	☐

CHALLENGING BIPOLAR WORKSHEEYT

OPEN

A NEW DAY AND AN EFFECTIVE PLAN WORKSHEET

Date :
....

Identify feelings, episodes of joy, excitement, strength or any
unusual talent that was part of your day , also things can you
do to prevent a full-blown (manic - depressive) episode

_____

_____

_____

_____

_____

_____

_____

_____

_____

_____

_____

_____

_____

_____

_____

_____

_____

DAILY BIPOLAR MOOD CYCLE

Instructions: Think about your day from start to finish. Color the first square to express your feelings each time of the day. Next, write a word that reflects your feelings, and draw in the circle a picture of your face that reflects your feelings at that moment.

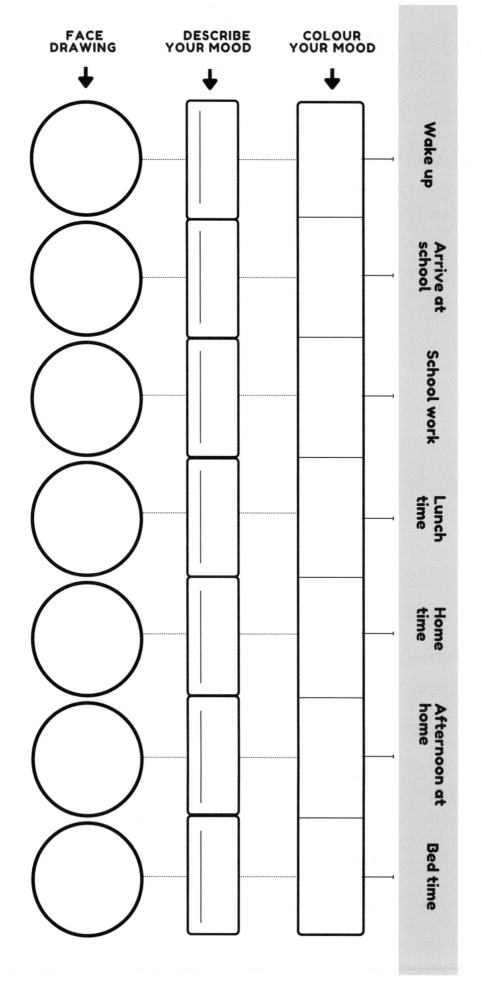

FACE DRAWING

DESCRIBE YOUR MOOD

COLOUR YOUR MOOD

Wake up

Arrive at school

School work

Lunch time

Home time

Afternoon at home

Bed time

BIPOLAR DISORDER
DBT WORKSHEET

MARK FEELINGS AND EPISODES OF JOY, EXCITEMENT, STRENGTH, OR ANY UNUSUAL TALENT THAT WERE PART OF YOUR DAY.

✓ ___ : ___

✓ ___ : ___

✓ ___ : ___

ONE WAY TO MAKE TOMORROW BETTER

Daily Mood Checker ✓

ANGRY	☐
ANNOYED	☐
ANXIOUS	☐
ASHAMED	☐
AWKWARD	☐
BRAVE	☐
CALM	☐
CHEERFUL	☐
CHILL	☐
CONFUSED	☐
DISCOURAGED	☐
DISTRACTED	☐
EMBARRASSED	☐
EXCITED	☐
FRIENDLY	☐
GUILTY	☐
HAPPY	☐
HOPEFUL	☐
LONELY	☐
LOVED	☐
NERVOUS	☐
OFFENDED	☐
SCARED	☐
THOUGHTFUL	☐
TIRED	☐
UNCOMFORTABLE	☐
UNSURE	☐

CHALLENGING BIPOLAR WORKSHEEYT

Date :
....

Identify feelings, episodes of joy, excitement, strength or any unusual talent that was part of your day , also things can you do to prevent a full-blown (manic - depressive) episode

_____

_____

_____

_____

_____

_____

_____

_____

_____

_____

_____

_____

_____

Delusions and Hallucinations, Paranoia Reflexions Tracker

Take care of your mental health. Know when to seek help.

(Symptom) or (Behavior)	Psychological and Physiological Reflexes
1	**2**
3	**4**
5	**6**
6	**6**
6	**6**
6	**6**

OVERCOMING BIPOLAR SYMPTOMS

IN THIS TABLE, TRY TO UNDERSTAND AND EXPLAIN THE EPISODES OF MANIA, DELUSIONS AND HALLUCINATIONS THAT OCCUR TO YOU FROM TIME TO TIME.
STATE THE EFFECT THEY HAVE ON YOUR FEELINGS AND ACTIONS, WHAT COPING SKILLS DO YOU THINK WORK WHEN YOU USE THEM, AND HOW SUCCESSFUL ARE YOU IN APPLYING THOSE SKILLS?

MANIC - DELUSIONS- HALLUCINATIONS EPISODES	COPING SKILLS USED OR PREVENTION METHODS

DAILY BIPOLAR MOOD CYCLE

Instructions: Think about your day from start to finish. Color the first square to express your feelings each time of the day. Next, write a word that reflects your feelings, and draw in the circle a picture of your face that reflects your feelings at that moment.

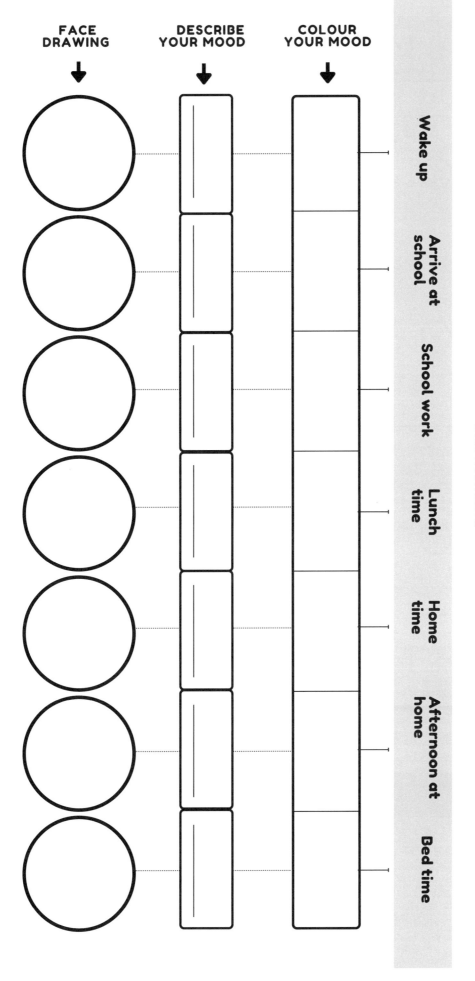

FACE DRAWING

DESCRIBE YOUR MOOD

COLOUR YOUR MOOD

Wake up

Arrive at school

School work

Lunch time

Home time

Afternoon at home

Bed time

BIPOLAR DISORDER DBT WORKSHEET

Date : / /

Sleep quality :

MARK FEELINGS AND EPISODES OF JOY, EXCITEMENT, STRENGTH, OR ANY UNUSUAL TALENT THAT WERE PART OF YOUR DAY.

✓ ___ : ___

✓ ___ : ___

✓ ___ : ___

ONE WAY TO MAKE TOMORROW BETTER

Daily Mood Checker ✔

ANGRY	☐
ANNOYED	☐
ANXIOUS	☐
ASHAMED	☐
AWKWARD	☐
BRAVE	☐
CALM	☐
CHEERFUL	☐
CHILL	☐
CONFUSED	☐
DISCOURAGED	☐
DISTRACTED	☐
EMBARRASSED	☐
EXCITED	☐
FRIENDLY	☐
GUILTY	☐
HAPPY	☐
HOPEFUL	☐
LONELY	☐
LOVED	☐
NERVOUS	☐
OFFENDED	☐
SCARED	☐
THOUGHTFUL	☐
TIRED	☐
UNCOMFORTABLE	☐
UNSURE	☐

CHALLENGING BIPOLAR WORKSHEEYT

A NEW DAY AND AN EFFECTIVE PLAN WORKSHEET

Date :
....

Identify feelings, episodes of joy, excitement, strength or any unusual talent that was part of your day , also things can you do to prevent a full-blown (manic - depressive) episode

_____

_____

_____

_____

_____

_____

_____

_____

_____

_____

_____

_____

_____

_____

DAILY BIPOLAR MOOD CYCLE

Instructions: Think about your day from start to finish. Color the first square to express your feelings each time of the day. Next, write a word that reflects your feelings, and draw in the circle a picture of your face that reflects your feelings at that moment.

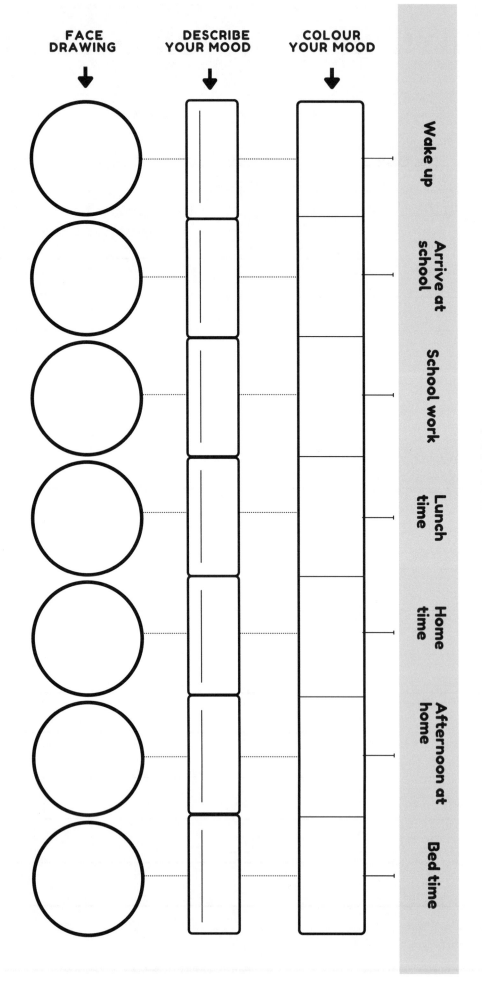

FACE DRAWING

DESCRIBE YOUR MOOD

COLOUR YOUR MOOD

Wake up

Arrive at school

School work

Lunch time

Home time

Afternoon at home

Bed time

BIPOLAR DISORDER
DBT WORKSHEET

MARK FEELINGS AND EPISODES OF JOY, EXCITEMENT, STRENGTH, OR ANY UNUSUAL TALENT THAT WERE PART OF YOUR DAY.

✓ ___ : ___

✓ ___ : ___

✓ ___ : ___

ONE WAY TO MAKE TOMORROW BETTER

Daily Mood Checker ✓

ANGRY	☐
ANNOYED	☐
ANXIOUS	☐
ASHAMED	☐
AWKWARD	☐
BRAVE	☐
CALM	☐
CHEERFUL	☐
CHILL	☐
CONFUSED	☐
DISCOURAGED	☐
DISTRACTED	☐
EMBARRASSED	☐
EXCITED	☐
FRIENDLY	☐
GUILTY	☐
HAPPY	☐
HOPEFUL	☐
LONELY	☐
LOVED	☐
NERVOUS	☐
OFFENDED	☐
SCARED	☐
THOUGHTFUL	☐
TIRED	☐
UNCOMFORTABLE	☐
UNSURE	☐

CHALLENGING BIPOLAR WORKSHEEYT

A NEW DAY AND AN EFFECTIVE PLAN WORKSHEET

Date :
....

Identify feelings, episodes of joy, excitement, strength or any
unusual talent that was part of your day , also things can you
do to prevent a full-blown (manic - depressive) episode

_____

_____

_____

_____

_____

_____

_____

_____

_____

_____

_____

_____

_____

Delusions and Hallucinations, Paranoia Reflexions Tracker

Take care of your mental health. Know when to seek help.

(Symptom) or (Behavior)	Psychological and Physiological Reflexes
1	2
3	4
5	6
6	6
6	6
6	6

OVERCOMING BIPOLAR SYMPTOMS

IN THIS TABLE, TRY TO UNDERSTAND AND EXPLAIN THE EPISODES OF MANIA, DELUSIONS AND HALLUCINATIONS THAT OCCUR TO YOU FROM TIME TO TIME.
STATE THE EFFECT THEY HAVE ON YOUR FEELINGS AND ACTIONS, WHAT COPING SKILLS DO YOU THINK WORK WHEN YOU USE THEM, AND HOW SUCCESSFUL ARE YOU IN APPLYING THOSE SKILLS?

MANIC - DELUSIONS- HALLUCINATIONS EPISODES	COPING SKILLS USED OR PREVENTION METHODS

DAILY BIPOLAR MOOD CYCLE

Instructions: Think about your day from start to finish. Color the first square to express your feelings each time of the day. Next, write a word that reflects your feelings, and draw in the circle a picture of your face that reflects your feelings at that moment.

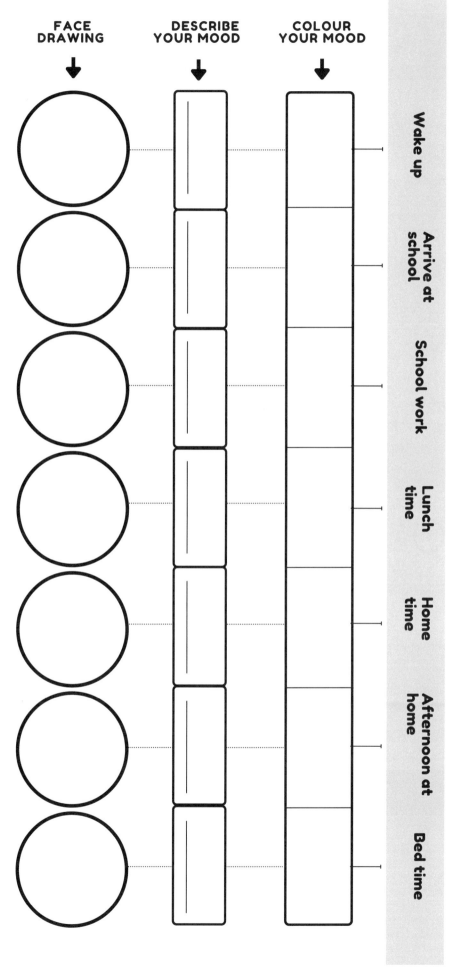

FACE DRAWING

DESCRIBE YOUR MOOD

COLOUR YOUR MOOD

Wake up

Arrive at school

School work

Lunch time

Home time

Afternoon at home

Bed time

BIPOLAR DISORDER
DBT WORKSHEET

Date : ⁣ / /

Sleep quality :

MARK FEELINGS AND EPISODES OF JOY, EXCITEMENT, STRENGTH, OR ANY UNUSUAL TALENT THAT WERE PART OF YOUR DAY.

✓ ___ : ___

✓ ___ : ___

✓ ___ : ___

ONE WAY TO MAKE TOMORROW BETTER

_____

_____

_____

Daily Mood Checker

Mood	
ANGRY	☐
ANNOYED	☐
ANXIOUS	☐
ASHAMED	☐
AWKWARD	☐
BRAVE	☐
CALM	☐
CHEERFUL	☐
CHILL	☐
CONFUSED	☐
DISCOURAGED	☐
DISTRACTED	☐
EMBARRASSED	☐
EXCITED	☐
FRIENDLY	☐
GUILTY	☐
HAPPY	☐
HOPEFUL	☐
LONELY	☐
LOVED	☐
NERVOUS	☐
OFFENDED	☐
SCARED	☐
THOUGHTFUL	☐
TIRED	☐
UNCOMFORTABLE	☐
UNSURE	☐

CHALLENGING BIPOLAR WORKSHEEYT

A NEW DAY AND AN EFFECTIVE PLAN WORKSHEET

Date :
....

Identify feelings, episodes of joy, excitement, strength or any unusual talent that was part of your day , also things can you do to prevent a full-blown (manic - depressive) episode

_____

_____

_____

_____

_____

_____

_____

_____

_____

_____

_____

_____

_____

_____

DAILY BIPOLAR MOOD CYCLE

Instructions: Think about your day from start to finish. Color the first square to express your feelings each time of the day. Next, write a word that reflects your feelings, and draw in the circle a picture of your face that reflects your feelings at that moment.

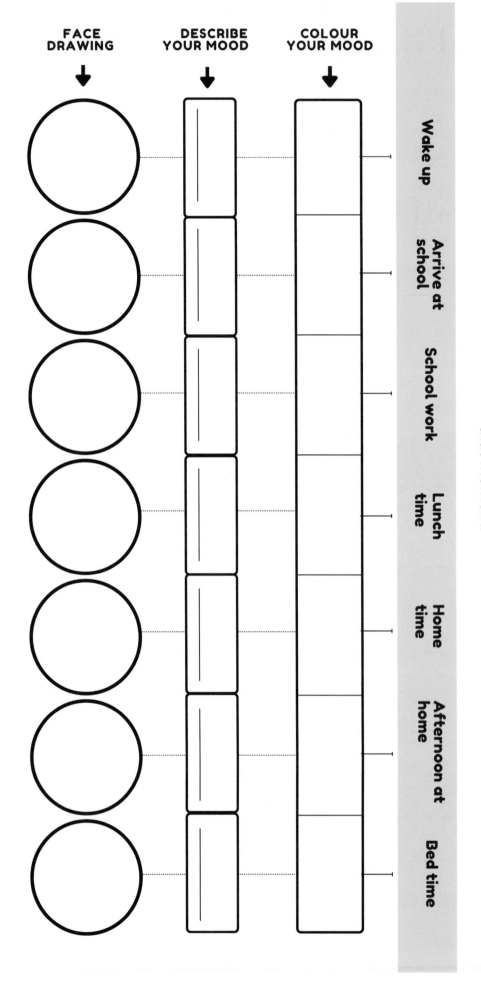

FACE DRAWING

DESCRIBE YOUR MOOD

COLOUR YOUR MOOD

Wake up

Arrive at school

School work

Lunch time

Home time

Afternoon at home

Bed time

BIPOLAR DISORDER
DBT WORKSHEET

MARK FEELINGS AND EPISODES OF JOY, EXCITEMENT, STRENGTH, OR ANY UNUSUAL TALENT THAT WERE PART OF YOUR DAY.

✓ ___ : ___

✓ ___ : ___

✓ ___ : ___

ONE WAY TO MAKE TOMORROW BETTER

Daily Mood Checker ✓

ANGRY	☐
ANNOYED	☐
ANXIOUS	☐
ASHAMED	☐
AWKWARD	☐
BRAVE	☐
CALM	☐
CHEERFUL	☐
CHILL	☐
CONFUSED	☐
DISCOURAGED	☐
DISTRACTED	☐
EMBARRASSED	☐
EXCITED	☐
FRIENDLY	☐
GUILTY	☐
HAPPY	☐
HOPEFUL	☐
LONELY	☐
LOVED	☐
NERVOUS	☐
OFFENDED	☐
SCARED	☐
THOUGHTFUL	☐
TIRED	☐
UNCOMFORTABLE	☐
UNSURE	☐

CHALLENGING BIPOLAR WORKSHEEYT

OPEN

Date :

_____

Identify feelings, episodes of joy, excitement, strength or any unusual talent that was part of your day , also things can you do to prevent a full-blown (manic - depressive) episode

_____

_____

_____

_____

_____

_____

_____

_____

_____

_____

_____

_____

_____

_____

Delusions and Hallucinations, Paranoia Reflexions Tracker

Take care of your mental health. Know when to seek help.

(Symptom) or (Behavior)	Psychological and Physiological Reflexes
1	**2**
3	**4**
5	**6**
6	**6**
6	**6**
6	**6**

OVERCOMING BIPOLAR SYMPTOMS

IN THIS TABLE, TRY TO UNDERSTAND AND EXPLAIN THE EPISODES OF MANIA, DELUSIONS AND HALLUCINATIONS THAT OCCUR TO YOU FROM TIME TO TIME.
STATE THE EFFECT THEY HAVE ON YOUR FEELINGS AND ACTIONS, WHAT COPING SKILLS DO YOU THINK WORK WHEN YOU USE THEM, AND HOW SUCCESSFUL ARE YOU IN APPLYING THOSE SKILLS?

MANIC - DELUSIONS- HALLUCINATIONS EPISODES	COPING SKILLS USED OR PREVENTION METHODS

DAILY BIPOLAR MOOD CYCLE

Instructions: Think about your day from start to finish. Color the first square to express your feelings each time of the day. Next, write a word that reflects your feelings, and draw in the circle a picture of your face that reflects your feelings at that moment.

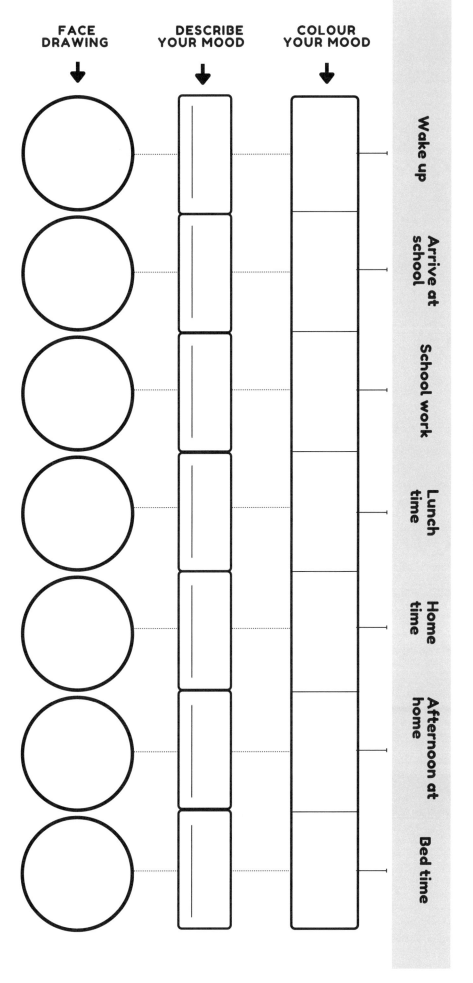

FACE DRAWING

DESCRIBE YOUR MOOD

COLOUR YOUR MOOD

- Wake up
- Arrive at school
- School work
- Lunch time
- Home time
- Afternoon at home
- Bed time

BIPOLAR DISORDER
DBT WORKSHEET

MARK FEELINGS AND EPISODES OF JOY, EXCITEMENT, STRENGTH, OR ANY UNUSUAL TALENT THAT WERE PART OF YOUR DAY.

✓ ___ : ___

✓ ___ : ___

✓ ___ : ___

ONE WAY TO MAKE TOMORROW BETTER

Daily Mood Checker ✓	
ANGRY	☐
ANNOYED	☐
ANXIOUS	☐
ASHAMED	☐
AWKWARD	☐
BRAVE	☐
CALM	☐
CHEERFUL	☐
CHILL	☐
CONFUSED	☐
DISCOURAGED	☐
DISTRACTED	☐
EMBARRASSED	☐
EXCITED	☐
FRIENDLY	☐
GUILTY	☐
HAPPY	☐
HOPEFUL	☐
LONELY	☐
LOVED	☐
NERVOUS	☐
OFFENDED	☐
SCARED	☐
THOUGHTFUL	☐
TIRED	☐
UNCOMFORTABLE	☐
UNSURE	☐

CHALLENGING BIPOLAR WORKSHEEYT

OPEN

Date :
....

Identify feelings, episodes of joy, excitement, strength or any
unusual talent that was part of your day , also things can you
do to prevent a full-blown (manic - depressive) episode

_____

_____

_____

_____

_____

_____

_____

_____

_____

_____

_____

_____

_____

_____

DAILY BIPOLAR MOOD CYCLE

Instructions: Think about your day from start to finish. Color the first square to express your feelings each time of the day. Next, write a word that reflects your feelings, and draw in the circle a picture of your face that reflects your feelings at that moment.

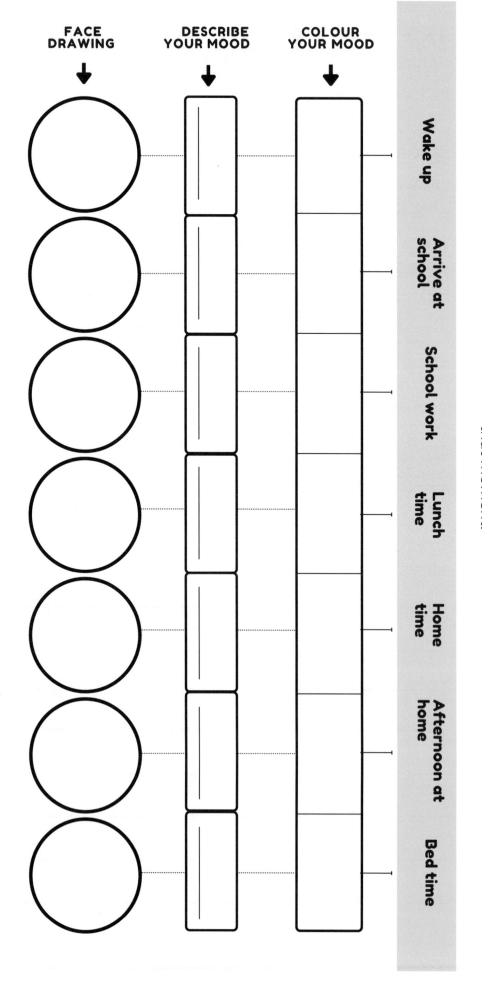

FACE DRAWING

DESCRIBE YOUR MOOD

COLOUR YOUR MOOD

Wake up

Arrive at school

School work

Lunch time

Home time

Afternoon at home

Bed time

BIPOLAR DISORDER
DBT WORKSHEET

MARK FEELINGS AND EPISODES OF JOY, EXCITEMENT, STRENGTH, OR ANY UNUSUAL TALENT THAT WERE PART OF YOUR DAY.

✓ ___ : ___

✓ ___ : ___

✓ ___ : ___

ONE WAY TO MAKE TOMORROW BETTER

Daily Mood Checker ✓

Mood	
ANGRY	☐
ANNOYED	☐
ANXIOUS	☐
ASHAMED	☐
AWKWARD	☐
BRAVE	☐
CALM	☐
CHEERFUL	☐
CHILL	☐
CONFUSED	☐
DISCOURAGED	☐
DISTRACTED	☐
EMBARRASSED	☐
EXCITED	☐
FRIENDLY	☐
GUILTY	☐
HAPPY	☐
HOPEFUL	☐
LONELY	☐
LOVED	☐
NERVOUS	☐
OFFENDED	☐
SCARED	☐
THOUGHTFUL	☐
TIRED	☐
UNCOMFORTABLE	☐
UNSURE	☐

CHALLENGING BIPOLAR WORKSHEEYT

Date :
....

Identify feelings, episodes of joy, excitement, strength or any unusual talent that was part of your day , also things can you do to prevent a full-blown (manic - depressive) episode

_____

_____

_____

_____

_____

_____

_____

_____

_____

_____

_____

_____

_____

Delusions and Hallucinations, Paranoia Reflexions Tracker

Take care of your mental health. Know when to seek help.

(Symptom) or (Behavior)	Psychological and Physiological Reflexes
1	**2**
3	**4**
5	**6**
6	**6**
6	**6**
6	**6**

OVERCOMING BIPOLAR SYMPTOMS

IN THIS TABLE, TRY TO UNDERSTAND AND EXPLAIN THE EPISODES OF MANIA, DELUSIONS AND HALLUCINATIONS THAT OCCUR TO YOU FROM TIME TO TIME.
STATE THE EFFECT THEY HAVE ON YOUR FEELINGS AND ACTIONS, WHAT COPING SKILLS DO YOU THINK WORK WHEN YOU USE THEM, AND HOW SUCCESSFUL ARE YOU IN APPLYING THOSE SKILLS?

MANIC - DELUSIONS- HALLUCINATIONS EPISODES	COPING SKILLS USED OR PREVENTION METHODS

DAILY BIPOLAR MOOD CYCLE

Instructions: Think about your day from start to finish. Color the first square to express your feelings each time of the day. Next, write a word that reflects your feelings, and draw in the circle a picture of your face that reflects your feelings at that moment.

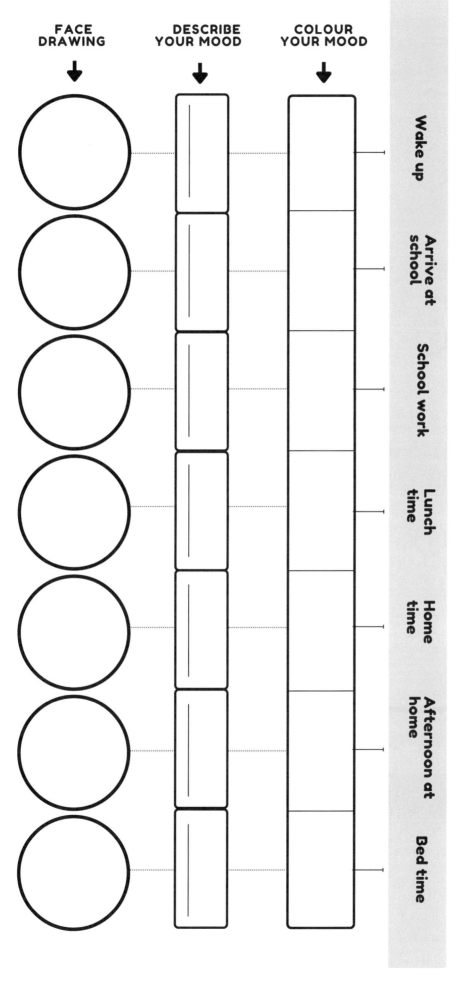

FACE DRAWING

DESCRIBE YOUR MOOD

COLOUR YOUR MOOD

Wake up

Arrive at school

School work

Lunch time

Home time

Afternoon at home

Bed time

BIPOLAR DISORDER
DBT WORKSHEET

MARK FEELINGS AND EPISODES OF JOY, EXCITEMENT, STRENGTH, OR ANY UNUSUAL TALENT THAT WERE PART OF YOUR DAY.

✓ —— : ——

✓ —— : ——

✓ —— : ——

ONE WAY TO MAKE TOMORROW BETTER

Daily Mood Checker ✔

ANGRY	☐
ANNOYED	☐
ANXIOUS	☐
ASHAMED	☐
AWKWARD	☐
BRAVE	☐
CALM	☐
CHEERFUL	☐
CHILL	☐
CONFUSED	☐
DISCOURAGED	☐
DISTRACTED	☐
EMBARRASSED	☐
EXCITED	☐
FRIENDLY	☐
GUILTY	☐
HAPPY	☐
HOPEFUL	☐
LONELY	☐
LOVED	☐
NERVOUS	☐
OFFENDED	☐
SCARED	☐
THOUGHTFUL	☐
TIRED	☐
UNCOMFORTABLE	☐
UNSURE	☐

CHALLENGING BIPOLAR WORKSHEEYT

Date :
....

Identify feelings, episodes of joy, excitement, strength or any unusual talent that was part of your day , also things can you do to prevent a full-blown (manic - depressive) episode

_____

_____

_____

_____

_____

_____

_____

_____

_____

_____

_____

_____

_____

OPEN

DAILY BIPOLAR MOOD CYCLE

Instructions: Think about your day from start to finish. Color the first square to express your feelings each time of the day. Next, write a word that reflects your feelings, and draw in the circle a picture of your face that reflects your feelings at that moment.

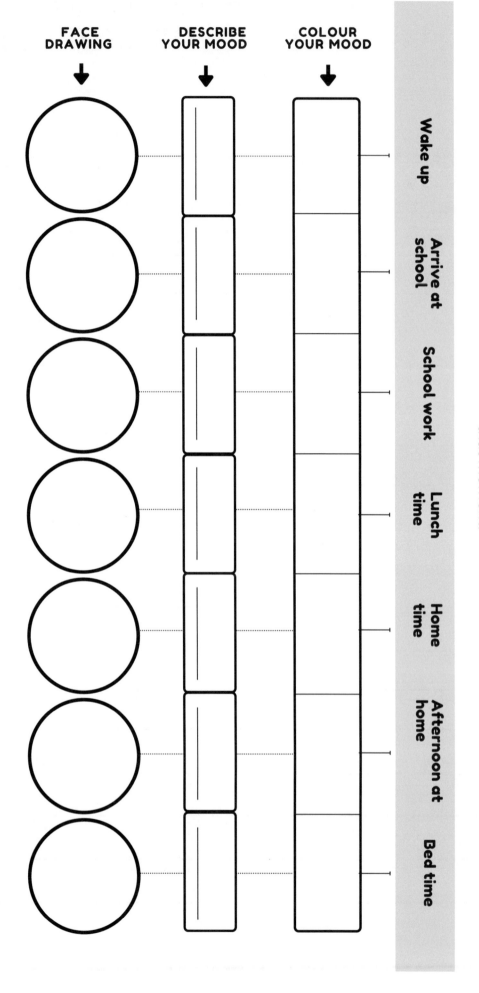

FACE DRAWING

DESCRIBE YOUR MOOD

COLOUR YOUR MOOD

Wake up

Arrive at school

School work

Lunch time

Home time

Afternoon at home

Bed time

BIPOLAR DISORDER
DBT WORKSHEET

MARK FEELINGS AND EPISODES OF JOY, EXCITEMENT, STRENGTH, OR ANY UNUSUAL TALENT THAT WERE PART OF YOUR DAY.

✓ ___ : ___

✓ ___ : ___

✓ ___ : ___

ONE WAY TO MAKE TOMORROW BETTER

Daily Mood Checker ✔

ANGRY	☐
ANNOYED	☐
ANXIOUS	☐
ASHAMED	☐
AWKWARD	☐
BRAVE	☐
CALM	☐
CHEERFUL	☐
CHILL	☐
CONFUSED	☐
DISCOURAGED	☐
DISTRACTED	☐
EMBARRASSED	☐
EXCITED	☐
FRIENDLY	☐
GUILTY	☐
HAPPY	☐
HOPEFUL	☐
LONELY	☐
LOVED	☐
NERVOUS	☐
OFFENDED	☐
SCARED	☐
THOUGHTFUL	☐
TIRED	☐
UNCOMFORTABLE	☐
UNSURE	☐

CHALLENGING BIPOLAR WORKSHEEYT

OPEN

Date :
....

Identify feelings, episodes of joy, excitement, strength or any unusual talent that was part of your day , also things can you do to prevent a full-blown (manic - depressive) episode

_____

_____

_____

_____

_____

_____

_____

_____

_____

_____

_____

_____

_____

_____

Delusions and Hallucinations, Paranoia Reflexions Tracker

Take care of your mental health. Know when to seek help.

(Symptom) or (Behavior)	Psychological and Physiological Reflexes
1	**2**
3	**4**
5	**6**
6	**6**
6	**6**
6	**6**

OVERCOMING BIPOLAR SYMPTOMS

IN THIS TABLE, TRY TO UNDERSTAND AND EXPLAIN THE EPISODES OF MANIA, DELUSIONS AND HALLUCINATIONS THAT OCCUR TO YOU FROM TIME TO TIME.
STATE THE EFFECT THEY HAVE ON YOUR FEELINGS AND ACTIONS, WHAT COPING SKILLS DO YOU THINK WORK WHEN YOU USE THEM, AND HOW SUCCESSFUL ARE YOU IN APPLYING THOSE SKILLS?

MANIC - DELUSIONS- HALLUCINATIONS EPISODES	COPING SKILLS USED OR PREVENTION METHODS

DAILY BIPOLAR MOOD CYCLE

Instructions: Think about your day from start to finish. Color the first square to express your feelings each time of the day. Next, write a word that reflects your feelings, and draw in the circle a picture of your face that reflects your feelings at that moment.

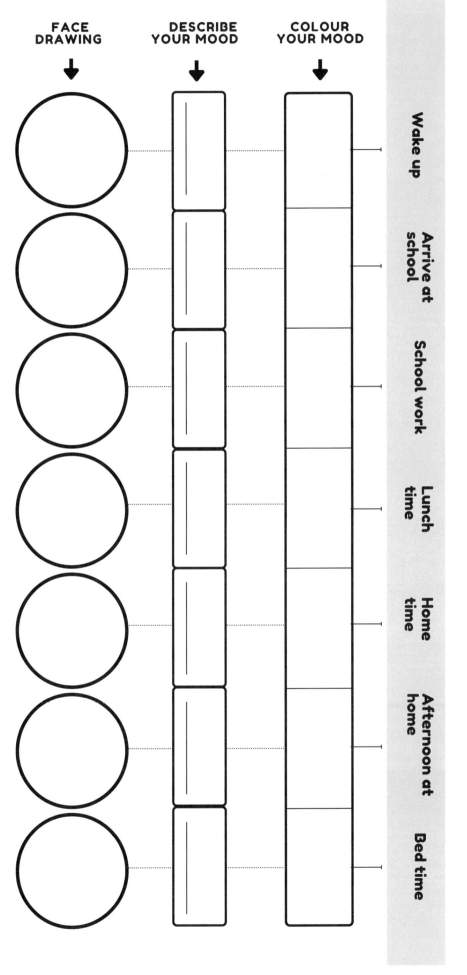

FACE DRAWING

DESCRIBE YOUR MOOD

COLOUR YOUR MOOD

Wake up

Arrive at school

School work

Lunch time

Home time

Afternoon at home

Bed time

BIPOLAR DISORDER
DBT WORKSHEET

Date : / /

Sleep quality :

MARK FEELINGS AND EPISODES OF JOY, EXCITEMENT, STRENGTH, OR ANY UNUSUAL TALENT THAT WERE PART OF YOUR DAY.

✓ ___ : ___

✓ ___ : ___

✓ ___ : ___

ONE WAY TO MAKE TOMORROW BETTER

Daily Mood Checker ✔

ANGRY	☐
ANNOYED	☐
ANXIOUS	☐
ASHAMED	☐
AWKWARD	☐
BRAVE	☐
CALM	☐
CHEERFUL	☐
CHILL	☐
CONFUSED	☐
DISCOURAGED	☐
DISTRACTED	☐
EMBARRASSED	☐
EXCITED	☐
FRIENDLY	☐
GUILTY	☐
HAPPY	☐
HOPEFUL	☐
LONELY	☐
LOVED	☐
NERVOUS	☐
OFFENDED	☐
SCARED	☐
THOUGHTFUL	☐
TIRED	☐
UNCOMFORTABLE	☐
UNSURE	☐

CHALLENGING BIPOLAR WORKSHEEYT

A NEW DAY AND AN EFFECTIVE PLAN WORKSHEET

Date :

....

Identify feelings, episodes of joy, excitement, strength or any unusual talent that was part of your day , also things can you do to prevent a full-blown (manic - depressive) episode

_____

_____

_____

_____

_____

_____

_____

_____

_____

_____

_____

_____

_____

_____

DAILY BIPOLAR MOOD CYCLE

Instructions: Think about your day from start to finish. Color the first square to express your feelings each time of the day. Next, write a word that reflects your feelings, and draw in the circle a picture of your face that reflects your feelings at that moment.

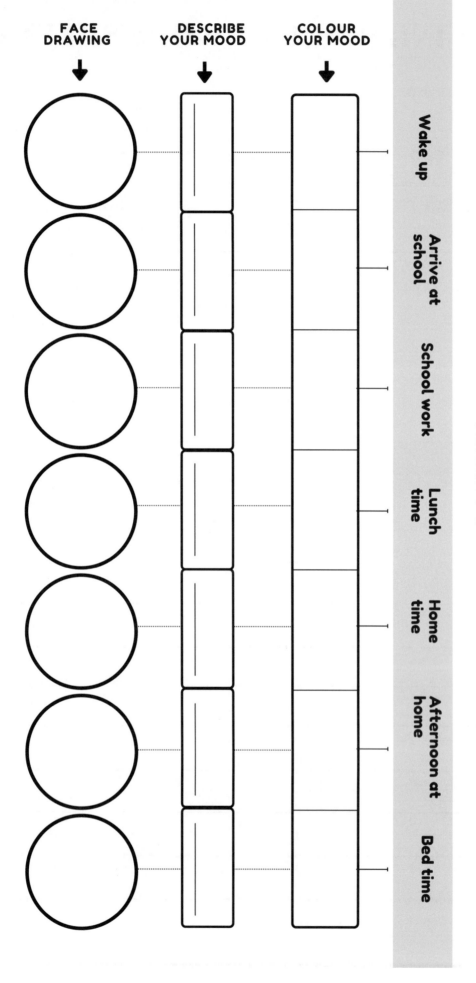

FACE DRAWING

DESCRIBE YOUR MOOD

COLOUR YOUR MOOD

- Wake up
- Arrive at school
- School work
- Lunch time
- Home time
- Afternoon at home
- Bed time

BIPOLAR DISORDER
DBT WORKSHEET

MARK FEELINGS AND EPISODES OF JOY, EXCITEMENT, STRENGTH, OR ANY UNUSUAL TALENT THAT WERE PART OF YOUR DAY.

Date : __ / __

Sleep quality :

Daily Mood Checker ✔

✓ __ : __

✓ __ : __

✓ __ : __

ONE WAY TO MAKE TOMORROW BETTER

ANGRY	☐
ANNOYED	☐
ANXIOUS	☐
ASHAMED	☐
AWKWARD	☐
BRAVE	☐
CALM	☐
CHEERFUL	☐
CHILL	☐
CONFUSED	☐
DISCOURAGED	☐
DISTRACTED	☐
EMBARRASSED	☐
EXCITED	☐
FRIENDLY	☐
GUILTY	☐
HAPPY	☐
HOPEFUL	☐
LONELY	☐
LOVED	☐
NERVOUS	☐
OFFENDED	☐
SCARED	☐
THOUGHTFUL	☐
TIRED	☐
UNCOMFORTABLE	☐
UNSURE	☐

CHALLENGING BIPOLAR WORKSHEEYT

A NEW DAY AND AN EFFECTIVE PLAN WORKSHEET

Date :

_____

Identify feelings, episodes of joy, excitement, strength or any
unusual talent that was part of your day , also things can you
do to prevent a full-blown (manic - depressive) episode

_____

_____

_____

_____

_____

_____

_____

_____

_____

_____

_____

_____

_____

Delusions and Hallucinations, Paranoia Reflexions Tracker

Take care of your mental health. Know when to seek help.

(Symptom) or (Behavior)	Psychological and Physiological Reflexes
1	**2**
3	**4**
5	**6**
6	**6**
6	**6**
6	**6**

OVERCOMING BIPOLAR SYMPTOMS

IN THIS TABLE, TRY TO UNDERSTAND AND EXPLAIN THE EPISODES OF MANIA, DELUSIONS AND HALLUCINATIONS THAT OCCUR TO YOU FROM TIME TO TIME.
STATE THE EFFECT THEY HAVE ON YOUR FEELINGS AND ACTIONS, WHAT COPING SKILLS DO YOU THINK WORK WHEN YOU USE THEM, AND HOW SUCCESSFUL ARE YOU IN APPLYING THOSE SKILLS?

MANIC - DELUSIONS- HALLUCINATIONS EPISODES	COPING SKILLS USED OR PREVENTION METHODS

DAILY BIPOLAR MOOD CYCLE

Instructions: Think about your day from start to finish. Color the first square to express your feelings each time of the day. Next, write a word that reflects your feelings, and draw in the circle a picture of your face that reflects your feelings at that moment.

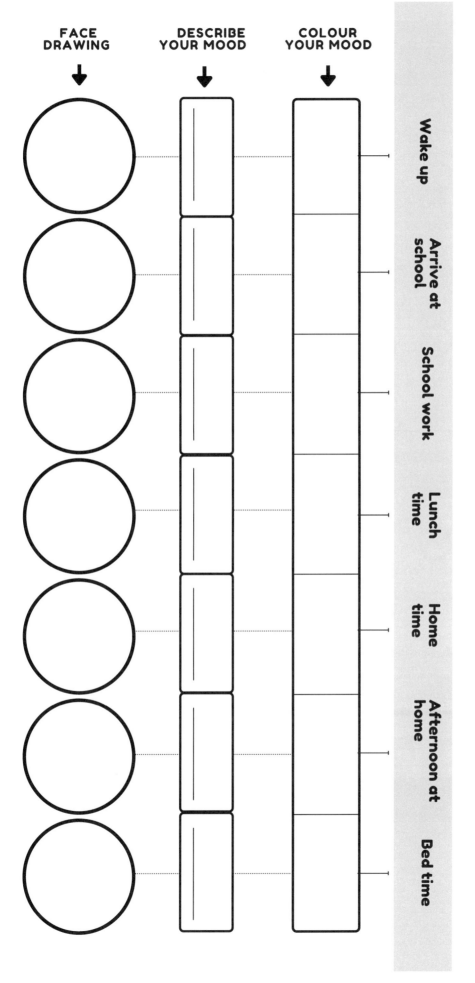

FACE DRAWING

DESCRIBE YOUR MOOD

COLOUR YOUR MOOD

Wake up

Arrive at school

School work

Lunch time

Home time

Afternoon at home

Bed time

BIPOLAR DISORDER
DBT WORKSHEET

MARK FEELINGS AND EPISODES OF JOY, EXCITEMENT, STRENGTH, OR ANY UNUSUAL TALENT THAT WERE PART OF YOUR DAY.

✓ ___ : ___

✓ ___ : ___

✓ ___ : ___

ONE WAY TO MAKE TOMORROW BETTER

Daily Mood Checker ✓

ANGRY	☐
ANNOYED	☐
ANXIOUS	☐
ASHAMED	☐
AWKWARD	☐
BRAVE	☐
CALM	☐
CHEERFUL	☐
CHILL	☐
CONFUSED	☐
DISCOURAGED	☐
DISTRACTED	☐
EMBARRASSED	☐
EXCITED	☐
FRIENDLY	☐
GUILTY	☐
HAPPY	☐
HOPEFUL	☐
LONELY	☐
LOVED	☐
NERVOUS	☐
OFFENDED	☐
SCARED	☐
THOUGHTFUL	☐
TIRED	☐
UNCOMFORTABLE	☐
UNSURE	☐

CHALLENGING BIPOLAR WORKSHEEYT

OPEN

Date :

_____

Identify feelings, episodes of joy, excitement, strength or any
unusual talent that was part of your day , also things can you
do to prevent a full-blown (manic - depressive) episode

_____

_____

_____

_____

_____

_____

_____

_____

_____

_____

_____

_____

_____

DAILY BIPOLAR MOOD CYCLE

Instructions: Think about your day from start to finish. Color the first square to express your feelings each time of the day. Next, write a word that reflects your feelings, and draw in the circle a picture of your face that reflects your feelings at that moment.

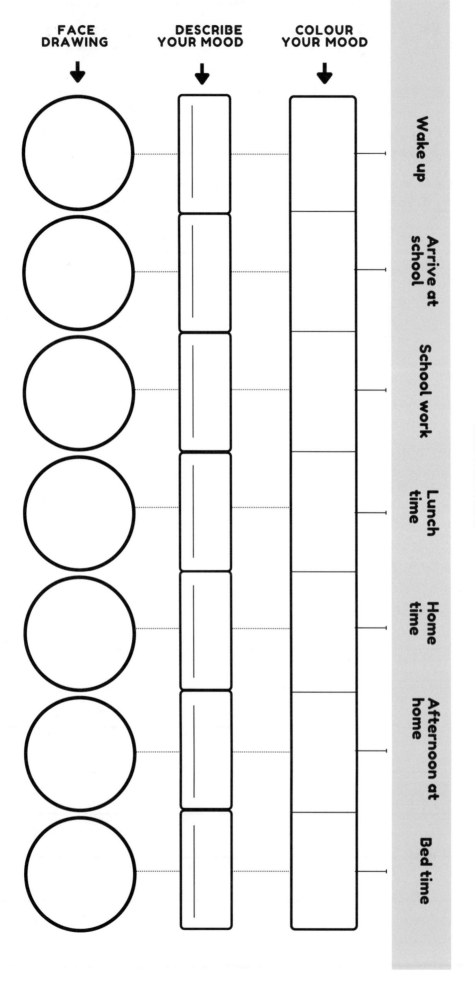

FACE DRAWING

DESCRIBE YOUR MOOD

COLOUR YOUR MOOD

Wake up

Arrive at school

School work

Lunch time

Home time

Afternoon at home

Bed time

BIPOLAR DISORDER
DBT WORKSHEET

MARK FEELINGS AND EPISODES OF JOY, EXCITEMENT, STRENGTH, OR ANY UNUSUAL TALENT THAT WERE PART OF YOUR DAY.

✓ ___ : ___

✓ ___ : ___

✓ ___ : ___

ONE WAY TO MAKE TOMORROW BETTER

Daily Mood Checker ✔

ANGRY	☐
ANNOYED	☐
ANXIOUS	☐
ASHAMED	☐
AWKWARD	☐
BRAVE	☐
CALM	☐
CHEERFUL	☐
CHILL	☐
CONFUSED	☐
DISCOURAGED	☐
DISTRACTED	☐
EMBARRASSED	☐
EXCITED	☐
FRIENDLY	☐
GUILTY	☐
HAPPY	☐
HOPEFUL	☐
LONELY	☐
LOVED	☐
NERVOUS	☐
OFFENDED	☐
SCARED	☐
THOUGHTFUL	☐
TIRED	☐
UNCOMFORTABLE	☐
UNSURE	☐

CHALLENGING BIPOLAR WORKSHEEYT

A NEW DAY AND AN EFFECTIVE PLAN WORKSHEET

Date :

_____

Identify feelings, episodes of joy, excitement, strength or any
unusual talent that was part of your day , also things can you
do to prevent a full-blown (manic - depressive) episode

_____

_____

_____

_____

_____

_____

_____

_____

_____

_____

_____

_____

_____

Delusions and Hallucinations, Paranoia Reflexions Tracker

Take care of your mental health. Know when to seek help.

(Symptom) or (Behavior)	Psychological and Physiological Reflexes
1	**2**
3	**4**
5	**6**
6	**6**
6	**6**
6	**6**

OVERCOMING BIPOLAR SYMPTOMS

IN THIS TABLE, TRY TO UNDERSTAND AND EXPLAIN THE EPISODES OF MANIA, DELUSIONS AND HALLUCINATIONS THAT OCCUR TO YOU FROM TIME TO TIME.
STATE THE EFFECT THEY HAVE ON YOUR FEELINGS AND ACTIONS, WHAT COPING SKILLS DO YOU THINK WORK WHEN YOU USE THEM, AND HOW SUCCESSFUL ARE YOU IN APPLYING THOSE SKILLS?

MANIC - DELUSIONS- HALLUCINATIONS EPISODES	COPING SKILLS USED OR PREVENTION METHODS

DAILY BIPOLAR MOOD CYCLE

Instructions: Think about your day from start to finish. Color the first square to express your feelings each time of the day. Next, write a word that reflects your feelings, and draw in the circle a picture of your face that reflects your feelings at that moment.

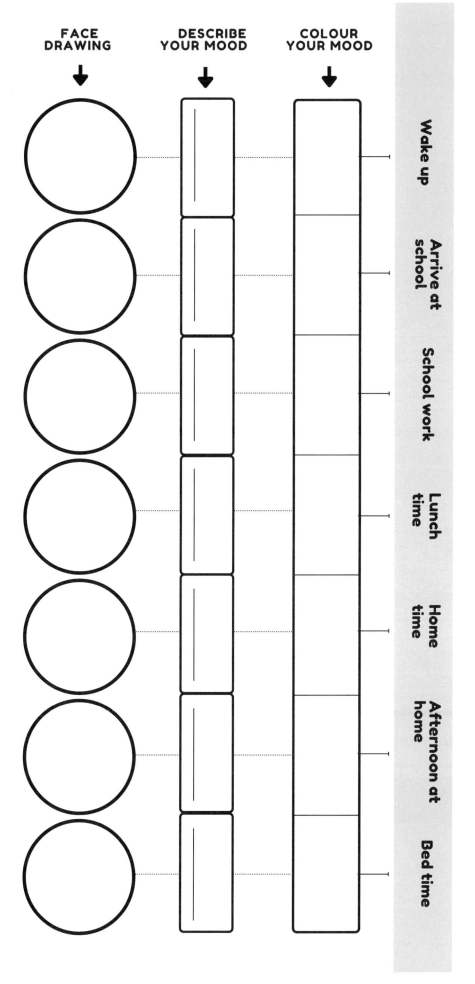

FACE DRAWING

DESCRIBE YOUR MOOD

COLOUR YOUR MOOD

Wake up

Arrive at school

School work

Lunch time

Home time

Afternoon at home

Bed time

BIPOLAR DISORDER
DBT WORKSHEET

MARK FEELINGS AND EPISODES OF JOY, EXCITEMENT, STRENGTH, OR ANY UNUSUAL TALENT THAT WERE PART OF YOUR DAY.

✓ ___ : ___

✓ ___ : ___

✓ ___ : ___

ONE WAY TO MAKE TOMORROW BETTER

Daily Mood Checker ✓

ANGRY	☐
ANNOYED	☐
ANXIOUS	☐
ASHAMED	☐
AWKWARD	☐
BRAVE	☐
CALM	☐
CHEERFUL	☐
CHILL	☐
CONFUSED	☐
DISCOURAGED	☐
DISTRACTED	☐
EMBARRASSED	☐
EXCITED	☐
FRIENDLY	☐
GUILTY	☐
HAPPY	☐
HOPEFUL	☐
LONELY	☐
LOVED	☐
NERVOUS	☐
OFFENDED	☐
SCARED	☐
THOUGHTFUL	☐
TIRED	☐
UNCOMFORTABLE	☐
UNSURE	☐

CHALLENGING BIPOLAR WORKSHEEYT

OPEN

Date :
....

Identify feelings, episodes of joy, excitement, strength or any
unusual talent that was part of your day , also things can you
do to prevent a full-blown (manic - depressive) episode

_____

_____

_____

_____

_____

_____

_____

_____

_____

_____

_____

_____

_____

DAILY BIPOLAR MOOD CYCLE

Instructions: Think about your day from start to finish. Color the first square to express your feelings each time of the day. Next, write a word that reflects your feelings, and draw in the circle a picture of your face that reflects your feelings at that moment.

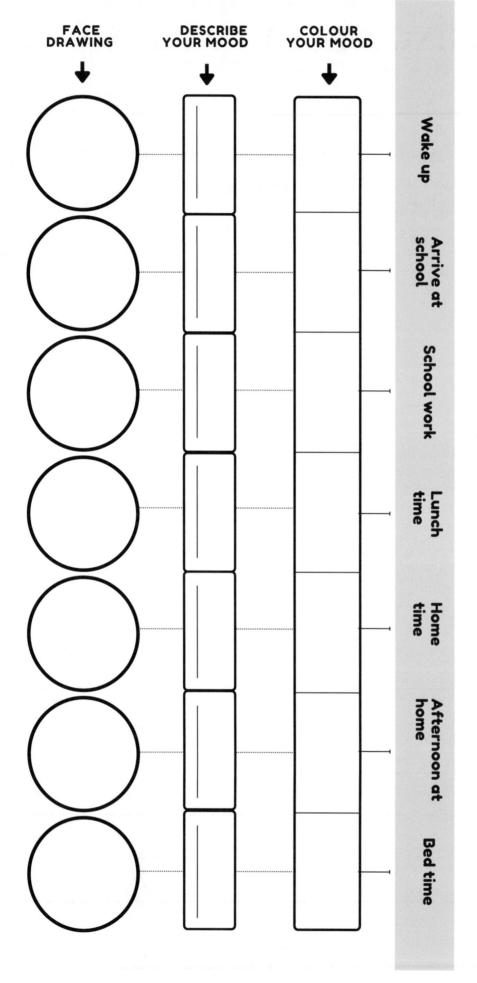

FACE DRAWING

DESCRIBE YOUR MOOD

COLOUR YOUR MOOD

Wake up

Arrive at school

School work

Lunch time

Home time

Afternoon at home

Bed time

BIPOLAR DISORDER
DBT WORKSHEET

MARK FEELINGS AND EPISODES OF JOY, EXCITEMENT, STRENGTH, OR ANY UNUSUAL TALENT THAT WERE PART OF YOUR DAY.

✓ ___ : ___

✓ ___ : ___

✓ ___ : ___

ONE WAY TO MAKE TOMORROW BETTER

Daily Mood Checker ✔

ANGRY	☐
ANNOYED	☐
ANXIOUS	☐
ASHAMED	☐
AWKWARD	☐
BRAVE	☐
CALM	☐
CHEERFUL	☐
CHILL	☐
CONFUSED	☐
DISCOURAGED	☐
DISTRACTED	☐
EMBARRASSED	☐
EXCITED	☐
FRIENDLY	☐
GUILTY	☐
HAPPY	☐
HOPEFUL	☐
LONELY	☐
LOVED	☐
NERVOUS	☐
OFFENDED	☐
SCARED	☐
THOUGHTFUL	☐
TIRED	☐
UNCOMFORTABLE	☐
UNSURE	☐

CHALLENGING BIPOLAR WORKSHEEYT

Date :
....

Identify feelings, episodes of joy, excitement, strength or any unusual talent that was part of your day , also things can you do to prevent a full-blown (manic - depressive) episode

_____

_____

_____

_____

_____

_____

_____

_____

_____

_____

_____

_____

_____

Delusions and Hallucinations, Paranoia Reflexions Tracker

Take care of your mental health. Know when to seek help.

(Symptom) or (Behavior)	Psychological and Physiological Reflexes
1	**2**
3	**4**
5	**6**
6	**6**
6	**6**
6	**6**

OVERCOMING BIPOLAR SYMPTOMS

IN THIS TABLE, TRY TO UNDERSTAND AND EXPLAIN THE EPISODES OF MANIA, DELUSIONS AND HALLUCINATIONS THAT OCCUR TO YOU FROM TIME TO TIME.
STATE THE EFFECT THEY HAVE ON YOUR FEELINGS AND ACTIONS, WHAT COPING SKILLS DO YOU THINK WORK WHEN YOU USE THEM, AND HOW SUCCESSFUL ARE YOU IN APPLYING THOSE SKILLS?

MANIC - DELUSIONS- HALLUCINATIONS EPISODES	COPING SKILLS USED OR PREVENTION METHODS

DAILY BIPOLAR MOOD CYCLE

Instructions: Think about your day from start to finish. Color the first square to express your feelings each time of the day. Next, write a word that reflects your feelings, and draw in the circle a picture of your face that reflects your feelings at that moment.

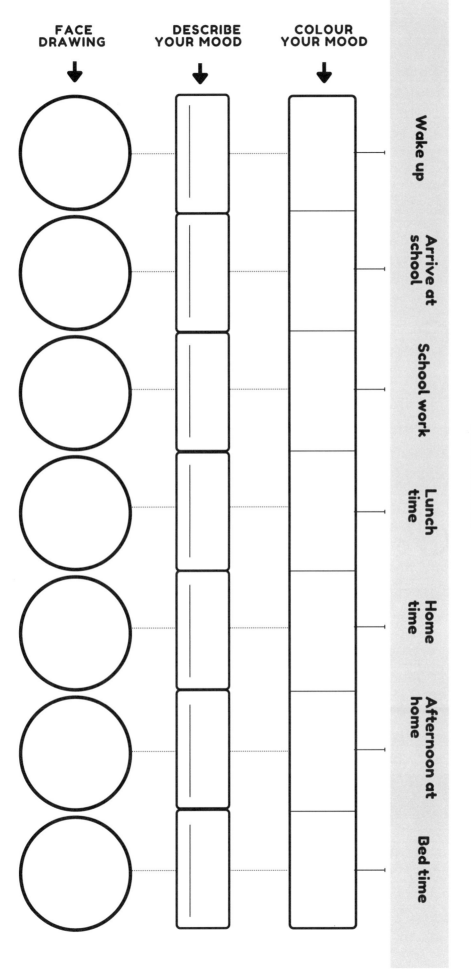

FACE DRAWING

DESCRIBE YOUR MOOD

COLOUR YOUR MOOD

Wake up

Arrive at school

School work

Lunch time

Home time

Afternoon at home

Bed time

BIPOLAR DISORDER DBT WORKSHEET

Date : __ / __

Sleep quality :

MARK FEELINGS AND EPISODES OF JOY, EXCITEMENT, STRENGTH, OR ANY UNUSUAL TALENT THAT WERE PART OF YOUR DAY.

✓ __ : __

✓ __ : __

✓ __ : __

ONE WAY TO MAKE TOMORROW BETTER

Daily Mood Checker ✓

ANGRY	☐
ANNOYED	☐
ANXIOUS	☐
ASHAMED	☐
AWKWARD	☐
BRAVE	☐
CALM	☐
CHEERFUL	☐
CHILL	☐
CONFUSED	☐
DISCOURAGED	☐
DISTRACTED	☐
EMBARRASSED	☐
EXCITED	☐
FRIENDLY	☐
GUILTY	☐
HAPPY	☐
HOPEFUL	☐
LONELY	☐
LOVED	☐
NERVOUS	☐
OFFENDED	☐
SCARED	☐
THOUGHTFUL	☐
TIRED	☐
UNCOMFORTABLE	☐
UNSURE	☐

CHALLENGING BIPOLAR WORKSHEEYT

OPEN

Date :

....

Identify feelings, episodes of joy, excitement, strength or any
unusual talent that was part of your day , also things can you
do to prevent a full-blown (manic - depressive) episode

_____

_____

_____

_____

_____

_____

_____

_____

_____

_____

_____

_____

_____

DAILY BIPOLAR MOOD CYCLE

Instructions: Think about your day from start to finish. Color the first square to express your feelings each time of the day. Next, write a word that reflects your feelings, and draw in the circle a picture of your face that reflects your feelings at that moment.

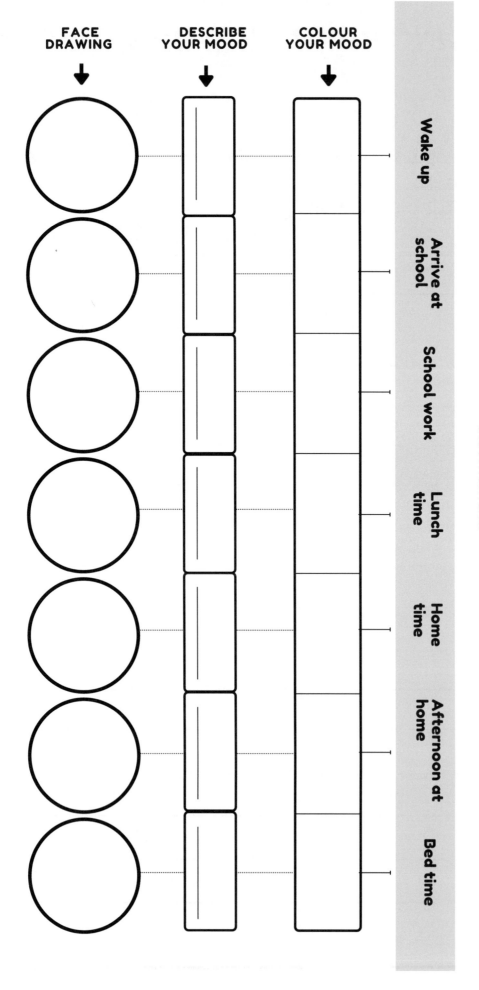

FACE DRAWING

DESCRIBE YOUR MOOD

COLOUR YOUR MOOD

Wake up

Arrive at school

School work

Lunch time

Home time

Afternoon at home

Bed time

BIPOLAR DISORDER
DBT WORKSHEET

MARK FEELINGS AND EPISODES OF JOY, EXCITEMENT, STRENGTH, OR ANY UNUSUAL TALENT THAT WERE PART OF YOUR DAY.

✓ ___ : ___

✓ ___ : ___

✓ ___ : ___

ONE WAY TO MAKE TOMORROW BETTER

Daily Mood Checker ✓

ANGRY	☐
ANNOYED	☐
ANXIOUS	☐
ASHAMED	☐
AWKWARD	☐
BRAVE	☐
CALM	☐
CHEERFUL	☐
CHILL	☐
CONFUSED	☐
DISCOURAGED	☐
DISTRACTED	☐
EMBARRASSED	☐
EXCITED	☐
FRIENDLY	☐
GUILTY	☐
HAPPY	☐
HOPEFUL	☐
LONELY	☐
LOVED	☐
NERVOUS	☐
OFFENDED	☐
SCARED	☐
THOUGHTFUL	☐
TIRED	☐
UNCOMFORTABLE	☐
UNSURE	☐

CHALLENGING BIPOLAR WORKSHEEYT

Date :
....

Identify feelings, episodes of joy, excitement, strength or any unusual talent that was part of your day , also things can you do to prevent a full-blown (manic - depressive) episode

_____

_____

_____

_____

_____

_____

_____

_____

_____

_____

_____

_____

Delusions and Hallucinations, Paranoia Reflexions Tracker

Take care of your mental health. Know when to seek help.

(Symptom) or (Behavior)	Psychological and Physiological Reflexes
1	**2**
3	**4**
5	**6**
6	**6**
6	**6**
6	**6**

OVERCOMING BIPOLAR SYMPTOMS

IN THIS TABLE, TRY TO UNDERSTAND AND EXPLAIN THE EPISODES OF MANIA, DELUSIONS AND HALLUCINATIONS THAT OCCUR TO YOU FROM TIME TO TIME.
STATE THE EFFECT THEY HAVE ON YOUR FEELINGS AND ACTIONS, WHAT COPING SKILLS DO YOU THINK WORK WHEN YOU USE THEM, AND HOW SUCCESSFUL ARE YOU IN APPLYING THOSE SKILLS?

MANIC - DELUSIONS- HALLUCINATIONS EPISODES	COPING SKILLS USED OR PREVENTION METHODS

DAILY BIPOLAR MOOD CYCLE

Instructions: Think about your day from start to finish. Color the first square to express your feelings each time of the day. Next, write a word that reflects your feelings, and draw in the circle a picture of your face that reflects your feelings at that moment.

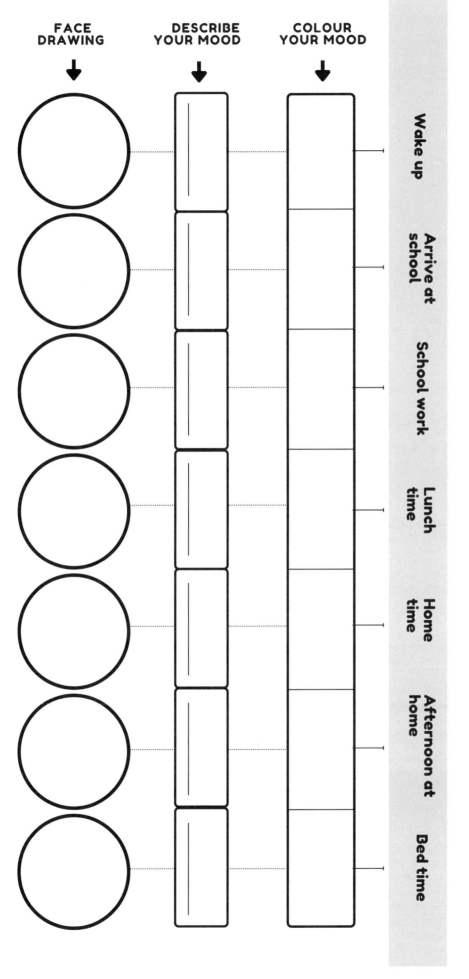

FACE DRAWING

DESCRIBE YOUR MOOD

COLOUR YOUR MOOD

Wake up

Arrive at school

School work

Lunch time

Home time

Afternoon at home

Bed time

BIPOLAR DISORDER
DBT WORKSHEET

Date : / /

Sleep quality :

MARK FEELINGS AND EPISODES OF JOY, EXCITEMENT, STRENGTH, OR ANY UNUSUAL TALENT THAT WERE PART OF YOUR DAY.

✔ ___ : ___

_____

_____

_____

✔ ___ : ___

_____

_____

_____

✔ ___ : ___

_____

_____

_____

ONE WAY TO MAKE TOMORROW BETTER

_____

_____

_____

Mood	
ANGRY	☐
ANNOYED	☐
ANXIOUS	☐
ASHAMED	☐
AWKWARD	☐
BRAVE	☐
CALM	☐
CHEERFUL	☐
CHILL	☐
CONFUSED	☐
DISCOURAGED	☐
DISTRACTED	☐
EMBARRASSED	☐
EXCITED	☐
FRIENDLY	☐
GUILTY	☐
HAPPY	☐
HOPEFUL	☐
LONELY	☐
LOVED	☐
NERVOUS	☐
OFFENDED	☐
SCARED	☐
THOUGHTFUL	☐
TIRED	☐
UNCOMFORTABLE	☐
UNSURE	☐

CHALLENGING BIPOLAR WORKSHEEYT

A NEW DAY AND AN EFFECTIVE PLAN WORKSHEET

OPEN

Date :

Identify feelings, episodes of joy, excitement, strength or any
unusual talent that was part of your day , also things can you
do to prevent a full-blown (manic - depressive) episode

_____

_____

_____

_____

_____

_____

_____

_____

_____

_____

_____

_____

_____

_____

DAILY BIPOLAR MOOD CYCLE

Instructions: Think about your day from start to finish. Color the first square to express your feelings each time of the day. Next, write a word that reflects your feelings, and draw in the circle a picture of your face that reflects your feelings at that moment.

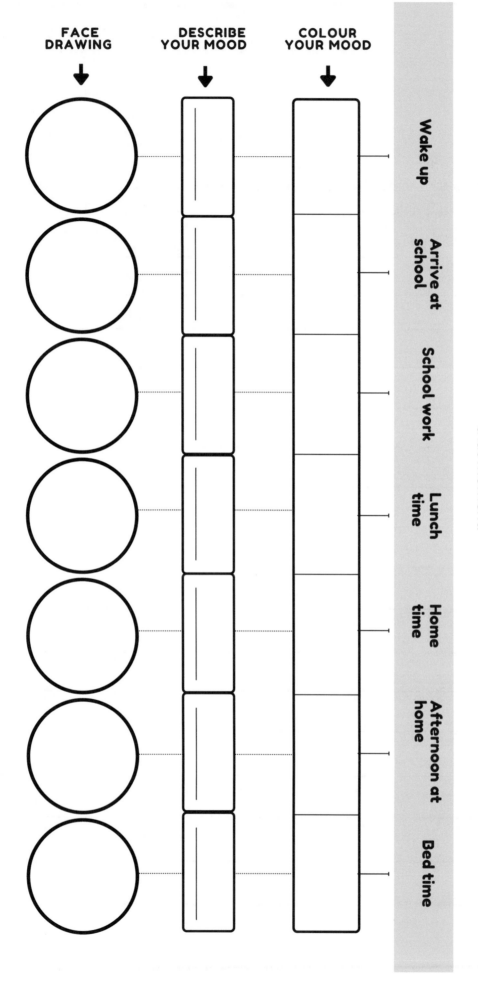

FACE DRAWING

DESCRIBE YOUR MOOD

COLOUR YOUR MOOD

Wake up

Arrive at school

School work

Lunch time

Home time

Afternoon at home

Bed time

BIPOLAR DISORDER
DBT WORKSHEET

MARK FEELINGS AND EPISODES OF JOY, EXCITEMENT, STRENGTH, OR ANY UNUSUAL TALENT THAT WERE PART OF YOUR DAY.

✓ ___ : ___

✓ ___ : ___

✓ ___ : ___

Daily Mood Checker ✓

- ANGRY ☐
- ANNOYED ☐
- ANXIOUS ☐
- ASHAMED ☐
- AWKWARD ☐
- BRAVE ☐
- CALM ☐
- CHEERFUL ☐
- CHILL ☐
- CONFUSED ☐
- DISCOURAGED ☐
- DISTRACTED ☐
- EMBARRASSED ☐
- EXCITED ☐
- FRIENDLY ☐
- GUILTY ☐
- HAPPY ☐
- HOPEFUL ☐
- LONELY ☐
- LOVED ☐
- NERVOUS ☐
- OFFENDED ☐
- SCARED ☐
- THOUGHTFUL ☐
- TIRED ☐
- UNCOMFORTABLE ☐
- UNSURE ☐

ONE WAY TO MAKE TOMORROW BETTER

CHALLENGING BIPOLAR WORKSHEEYT

Date :
....

Identify feelings, episodes of joy, excitement, strength or any unusual talent that was part of your day , also things can you do to prevent a full-blown (manic - depressive) episode

_____

_____

_____

_____

_____

_____

_____

_____

_____

_____

_____

_____

_____

_____

Delusions and Hallucinations, Paranoia Reflexions Tracker

Take care of your mental health. Know when to seek help.

(Symptom) or (Behavior)	Psychological and Physiological Reflexes
1	**2**
3	**4**
5	**6**
6	**6**
6	**6**
6	**6**

OVERCOMING BIPOLAR SYMPTOMS

IN THIS TABLE, TRY TO UNDERSTAND AND EXPLAIN THE EPISODES OF MANIA, DELUSIONS AND HALLUCINATIONS THAT OCCUR TO YOU FROM TIME TO TIME.
STATE THE EFFECT THEY HAVE ON YOUR FEELINGS AND ACTIONS, WHAT COPING SKILLS DO YOU THINK WORK WHEN YOU USE THEM, AND HOW SUCCESSFUL ARE YOU IN APPLYING THOSE SKILLS?

MANIC - DELUSIONS- HALLUCINATIONS EPISODES	COPING SKILLS USED OR PREVENTION METHODS

DAILY BIPOLAR MOOD CYCLE

Instructions: Think about your day from start to finish. Color the first square to express your feelings each time of the day. Next, write a word that reflects your feelings, and draw in the circle a picture of your face that reflects your feelings at that moment.

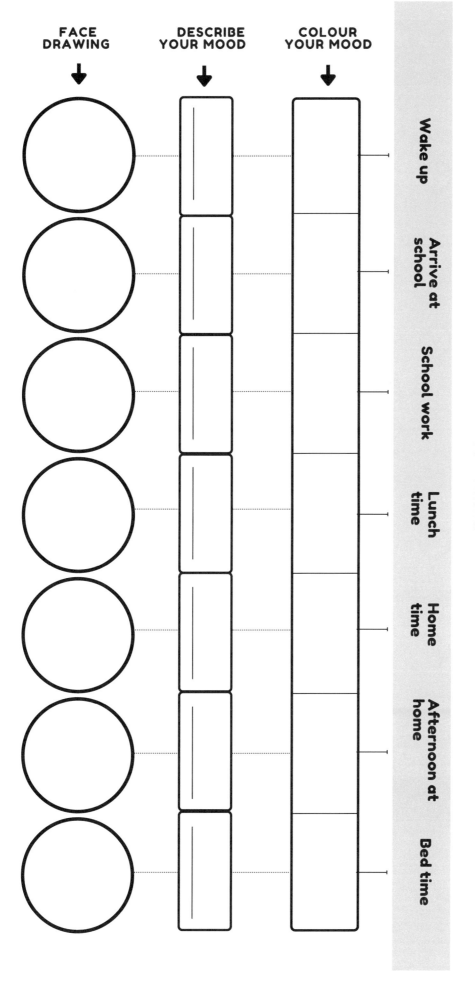

FACE DRAWING

DESCRIBE YOUR MOOD

COLOUR YOUR MOOD

Wake up

Arrive at school

School work

Lunch time

Home time

Afternoon at home

Bed time

BIPOLAR DISORDER
DBT WORKSHEET

MARK FEELINGS AND EPISODES OF JOY, EXCITEMENT, STRENGTH, OR ANY UNUSUAL TALENT THAT WERE PART OF YOUR DAY.

✓ ___ : ___

_____

_____

✓ ___ : ___

_____

_____

_____

✓ ___ : ___

_____

_____

_____

Daily Mood Checker ✔

ANGRY	☐
ANNOYED	☐
ANXIOUS	☐
ASHAMED	☐
AWKWARD	☐
BRAVE	☐
CALM	☐
CHEERFUL	☐
CHILL	☐
CONFUSED	☐
DISCOURAGED	☐
DISTRACTED	☐
EMBARRASSED	☐
EXCITED	☐
FRIENDLY	☐
GUILTY	☐
HAPPY	☐
HOPEFUL	☐
LONELY	☐
LOVED	☐
NERVOUS	☐
OFFENDED	☐
SCARED	☐
THOUGHTFUL	☐
TIRED	☐
UNCOMFORTABLE	☐
UNSURE	☐

ONE WAY TO MAKE TOMORROW BETTER

_____

_____

_____

CHALLENGING BIPOLAR WORKSHEEYT

Date :
....

Identify feelings, episodes of joy, excitement, strength or any unusual talent that was part of your day , also things can you do to prevent a full-blown (manic - depressive) episode

_____

_____

_____

_____

_____

_____

_____

_____

_____

_____

_____

_____

_____

DAILY BIPOLAR MOOD CYCLE

Instructions: Think about your day from start to finish. Color the first square to express your feelings each time of the day. Next, write a word that reflects your feelings, and draw in the circle a picture of your face that reflects your feelings at that moment.

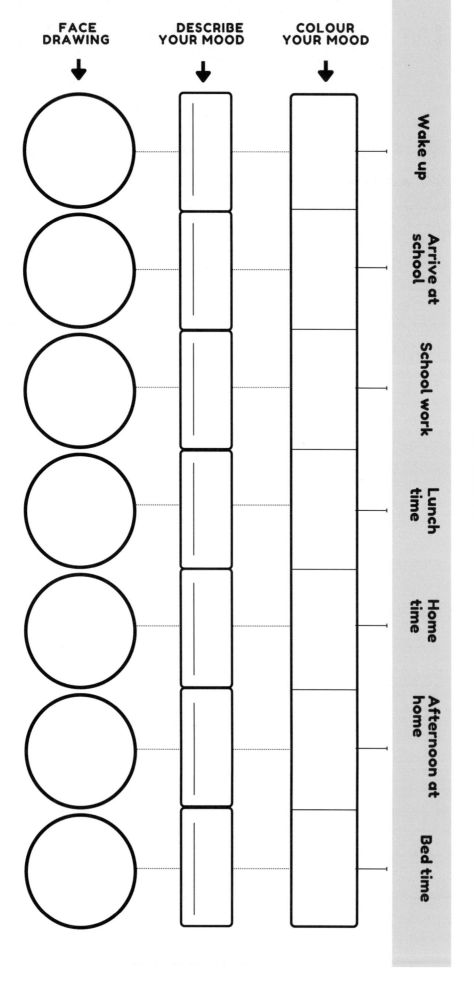

FACE DRAWING

DESCRIBE YOUR MOOD

COLOUR YOUR MOOD

Wake up

Arrive at school

School work

Lunch time

Home time

Afternoon at home

Bed time

BIPOLAR DISORDER DBT WORKSHEET

MARK FEELINGS AND EPISODES OF JOY, EXCITEMENT, STRENGTH, OR ANY UNUSUAL TALENT THAT WERE PART OF YOUR DAY.

✓ ___ : ___

✓ ___ : ___

✓ ___ : ___

ONE WAY TO MAKE TOMORROW BETTER

Daily Mood Checker ✓

ANGRY	☐
ANNOYED	☐
ANXIOUS	☐
ASHAMED	☐
AWKWARD	☐
BRAVE	☐
CALM	☐
CHEERFUL	☐
CHILL	☐
CONFUSED	☐
DISCOURAGED	☐
DISTRACTED	☐
EMBARRASSED	☐
EXCITED	☐
FRIENDLY	☐
GUILTY	☐
HAPPY	☐
HOPEFUL	☐
LONELY	☐
LOVED	☐
NERVOUS	☐
OFFENDED	☐
SCARED	☐
THOUGHTFUL	☐
TIRED	☐
UNCOMFORTABLE	☐
UNSURE	☐

CHALLENGING BIPOLAR WORKSHEEYT

Date :
....

Identify feelings, episodes of joy, excitement, strength or any unusual talent that was part of your day , also things can you do to prevent a full-blown (manic - depressive) episode

_____

_____

_____

_____

_____

_____

_____

_____

_____

_____

_____

_____

_____

_____

Delusions and Hallucinations, Paranoia Reflexions Tracker

Take care of your mental health. Know when to seek help.

(Symptom) or (Behavior)	Psychological and Physiological Reflexes
1	**2**
3	**4**
5	**6**
6	**6**
6	**6**
6	**6**

OVERCOMING BIPOLAR SYMPTOMS

IN THIS TABLE, TRY TO UNDERSTAND AND EXPLAIN THE EPISODES OF MANIA, DELUSIONS AND HALLUCINATIONS THAT OCCUR TO YOU FROM TIME TO TIME.
STATE THE EFFECT THEY HAVE ON YOUR FEELINGS AND ACTIONS, WHAT COPING SKILLS DO YOU THINK WORK WHEN YOU USE THEM, AND HOW SUCCESSFUL ARE YOU IN APPLYING THOSE SKILLS?

MANIC - DELUSIONS- HALLUCINATIONS EPISODES	COPING SKILLS USED OR PREVENTION METHODS

DAILY BIPOLAR MOOD CYCLE

Instructions: Think about your day from start to finish. Color the first square to express your feelings each time of the day. Next, write a word that reflects your feelings, and draw in the circle a picture of your face that reflects your feelings at that moment.

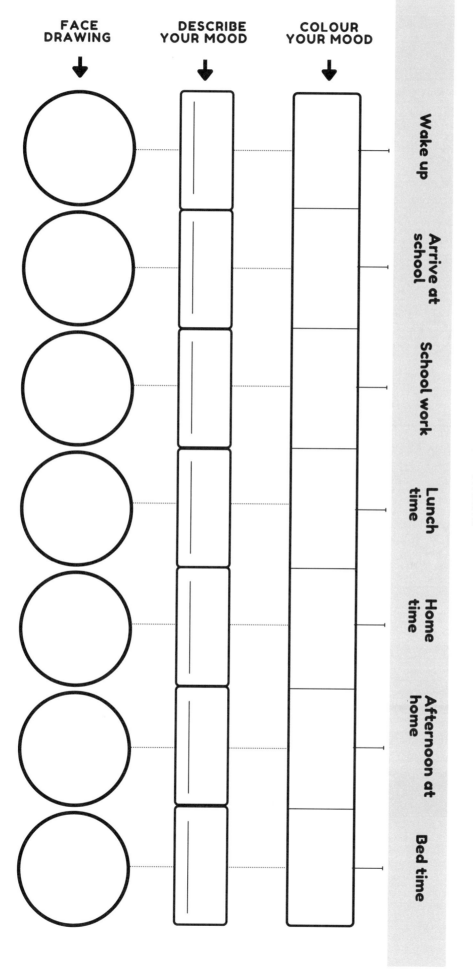

FACE DRAWING

DESCRIBE YOUR MOOD

COLOUR YOUR MOOD

Wake up

Arrive at school

School work

Lunch time

Home time

Afternoon at home

Bed time

BIPOLAR DISORDER
DBT WORKSHEET

MARK FEELINGS AND EPISODES OF JOY, EXCITEMENT, STRENGTH, OR ANY UNUSUAL TALENT THAT WERE PART OF YOUR DAY.

✓ ___ : ___

✓ ___ : ___

✓ ___ : ___

ONE WAY TO MAKE TOMORROW BETTER

Daily Mood Checker ✓

ANGRY	☐
ANNOYED	☐
ANXIOUS	☐
ASHAMED	☐
AWKWARD	☐
BRAVE	☐
CALM	☐
CHEERFUL	☐
CHILL	☐
CONFUSED	☐
DISCOURAGED	☐
DISTRACTED	☐
EMBARRASSED	☐
EXCITED	☐
FRIENDLY	☐
GUILTY	☐
HAPPY	☐
HOPEFUL	☐
LONELY	☐
LOVED	☐
NERVOUS	☐
OFFENDED	☐
SCARED	☐
THOUGHTFUL	☐
TIRED	☐
UNCOMFORTABLE	☐
UNSURE	☐

CHALLENGING BIPOLAR WORKSHEEYT

OPEN

Date :

....

Identify feelings, episodes of joy, excitement, strength or any
unusual talent that was part of your day , also things can you
do to prevent a full-blown (manic - depressive) episode

_____

_____

_____

_____

_____

_____

_____

_____

_____

_____

_____

_____

_____

_____

DAILY BIPOLAR MOOD CYCLE

Instructions: Think about your day from start to finish. Color the first square to express your feelings each time of the day. Next, write a word that reflects your feelings, and draw in the circle a picture of your face that reflects your feelings at that moment.

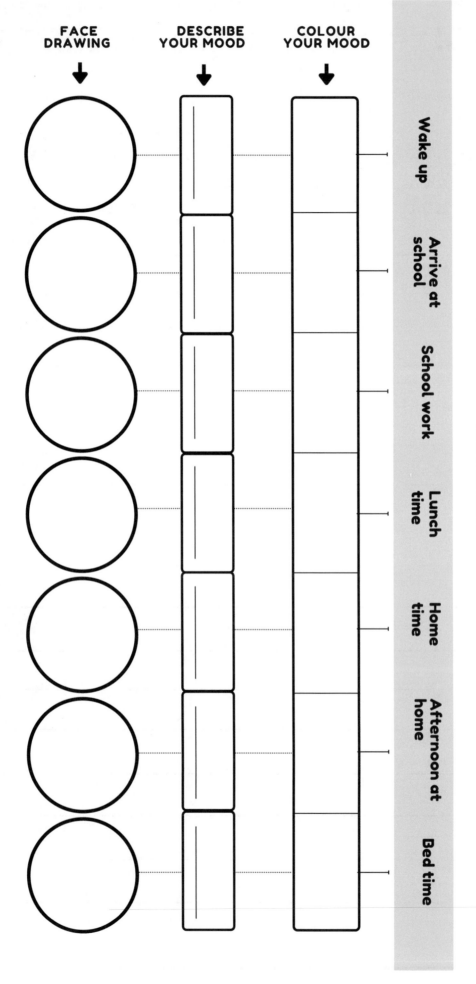

FACE DRAWING

DESCRIBE YOUR MOOD

COLOUR YOUR MOOD

- Wake up
- Arrive at school
- School work
- Lunch time
- Home time
- Afternoon at home
- Bed time

Made in United States
Troutdale, OR
02/05/2024

17472240R00058